WITHDRAWN
UTSA LIBRARIES

RENEWALS 458-4574

| DATE DUE | | | |
|---|---|---|---|
| AUG 05 | | | |
| | | | |
| | | | |
| | | | |
| | | | |
| | | | |
| | | | |
| | | | |
| | | | |
| | | | |
| | | | |
| | | | |
| | | | |
| | | | |
| | | | |
| | | | |
| | | | |
| GAYLORD | | | PRINTED IN U.S.A |

Rooms, Which Were People

## The Ohio State University Press / *The Journal* Award in Poetry
David Citino, Poetry Editor

| | | |
|---|---|---|
| 1989 | Albert Goldbarth | *Popular Culture* |
| 1988 | Sue Owen | *The Book of Winter* |
| 1987 | Robert Cording | *Life-list* |

## The George Elliston Poetry Prize

| | | |
|---|---|---|
| 1987 | Walter McDonald | *The Flying Dutchman* |
| 1986 | David Weiss | *The Fourth Part of the World* |
| 1985 | David Bergman | *Cracking the Code* |

## International Poetry from Ohio State University Press

*At the Court of Yearning*
Lucian Blaga
Translated from the Romanian and Introduced by Andrei Codrescu
Afterword by Marcel Cornis-Pop

*The Eyesight of Wasps*
Osip Mandelshtam
Translated from the Russian by James Greene

*Contemporary Indian Poetry*
Edited by Kaiser Haq

# Rooms, Which Were People

Winner of the 1990
Ohio State University Press / *The Journal* Award in Poetry

## Mary Cross

Ohio State University Press
*Columbus*

Copyright © 1990 by the Ohio State University Press.
All rights reserved.

Library of Congress Cataloging-in-Publication Data

Cross, Mary, 1958–
    Rooms, which were people  /  Mary Cross.
        p.    cm.
    "Winner of the 1990 Ohio State University Press/The Journal
award in poetry."
    ISBN 0–8142–0532–1 (alk. paper).–ISBN 0–8142–0533–X
(pbk. :  alk. paper)
    I. Title.
PS3553.R5724R6        1990
811'.54–dc20                                                    90–7415
                                                                  CIP

    ⊗  The paper in this book meets the guidelines for permanence
and durability of the Committee on Production Guidelines for
Book Longevity of the Council on Library Resources.

Printed in the U.S.A.

9 8 7 6 5 4 3 2 1

"When will you stop asking so much of life, Irène?"
*A Sunday in the Country*

# Acknowledgments

The author gratefully acknowledges the following publications in which poems from this book first appeared:

*American Poetry Review:* "Reckoning with the Sheep," "Bodies Subject to Its Action"

*Ascent:* "Whisper," "Nothing Passes Away"

*Ironwood:* "3rd Coast Café"

*Madison Review:* "Burning in Green"

*Ohio Review* (the following poems appeared in a chapbook entitled *Vis-à-vis*): "Never a Singular Happening," "Evidence for a Love Poem," "Architecture of an Affair," "Fear," "The Integrity of Pigeons," "In Order to Get Up," "Toward a Common Conclusion," "In the Same Breath," "Ponder the Motion," "February 10th," "Andante"

*Pavement:* "At a Distance," "When the Band Plays," "Elsewhereness"

*Ploughshares:* "I Am Told"

The author would like to thank the Ragdale Foundation for a residency that contributed to the completion of this book.

Special thanks to the Brown Street contingent for their endless support and enchantment.

*for my mother,*
*Lorraine Margaret Cross*

*and for my grandmother,*
*Catherine Adeline Cross*
*1889–1983*

# Contents

## Bodies Subject to Its Action

# Burning in Green

# Driver,

Tell me two stars, three goats outside my door,
the cock that rotates its neck in the backyard,
are not real.
Tell me, with your enormous icon glued to the windshield,
as you let me go in the whoosh that opens the bus door,
that we are strangers.
Look at me through sunglass filters,
through your punctual bus schedule,
through your oversized rearview mirror—
and you will see a woman examining the silver fastener
on the strap she holds to keep herself in place,
steady, in the aisle.
She braces herself against someone's knee.
Everything she sees, she sees through windows,
open and closed—
all of it passing, changing,
without her, into the blue sun-scorched roofs,
into the sky, into the white crosses
of the 365 churches on the island of Sifnos.

She is almost there.
She is almost gone.
Outside, an animal in midair
is trying to bite off a leaf from an olive tree.
It doesn't get it.
It never will. She thinks distance
is simply the space between here and there.

You think she may not have a lover.
She may prefer to be alone.
Occasionally you catch her eye, ephemeral,
in the gray mirror.
The heat, in an hour or so,
will create a mirage in front of you,

a wavelike puddle; she will be pushing her hair
away from her face, the animal's neck
will continue to strain upward,
mouth open. It is the straining you see,
the memory of, the fear of knowing

I am your passenger
where symbols, maps, tacked points of interest,
have a way of looking exactly as they are—
as they appear casually on paper, in longhand,
in photograph, in the large space
of world or country.

# Burning in Green

If you want to stand by the window, then
watch the lady in a blue skirt and white blouse
walk to work. Think of her hands wiping the bar,
the way she smacks her hips when she laughs.
Three hundred and fifty miles from here
my sister solders a blue wire onto a circuit board.
None of us is alone.

The Hot l Warren is hot with two ballplayers
spitting their beer through words, pointing
fingers at chests they've never seen.
Livvy talks to herself in her room
like she's reading the cover of a book.
Someone is taking a bath upstairs.

Don't let your blue walls get in the way,
unbutton your jeans, put your lips on my belly,
and sip, Honey, sip that Rolling Rock
and let me taste it from your mouth. Outside,
this Iowa landscape is burning in green
till it hurts.

Let the angels look at us through bamboo shades
and describe our skin like the soil off Highway 1,
how it turns from black to red.
Let them see our hands sift through hands,
through hair, the way nothing stops.


*to B.*

# Toward a Common Conclusion

That is to say *I am* watching the sea lions feed
on trout, swallow up head and tail
like an anesthesized mouth
picking up tongue to chew.
Hear the thug?
Oh-how-pretty-we-are in the brain.
Watch that one.
He'll get it before the keeper has a chance
to call, to slap fish
down on concrete.

Maybe we never know if we are changed.
How you're there, and not there.

Once on the back of a motorcycle
a boy rode no-hands
to tell me he was happy.
So much distortion in a person's reflection,
how the land sees you
from the fishnet finish of a helmet.
I remember we stopped.
He sang a song about a river
and the people who lived there . . .
*what about me / what about me*
they asked.

# Cross-Country

In Reno a truck stop sports
neon and slot-machine bells
the length of a gymnasium.
In Mexico the fat of your hand, slammed
on the corner of a table, swells—
your friend watches you
witness your own bruise.
You say you're a series of conclusions.
There are salt flats near Salt Lake,
how white, how cool
for a second.
The moon comes out like salsa. Your feet
rest on the indoor-outdoor carpeting.
You want to drive your car that won't do
more than 25 at 11,000 feet,
and it's burning oil.
This is what you are at 3 A.M.
This is what you must have been,
cashier in Utah, when you shot

jackrabbits from the hood of a jeep—
how many an hour?
This is what we are
when we cannot buy the pig
the Indian woman sells
under a straw roof on 1-D.
This is what we hear:
three taps and the shoemaker in Ensenada
heels another cowboy boot.
His baby lies on the couch,

the nipple of the bottle
barely touching the teeth.
Your friend takes a picture.
The shoemaker smiles.
The baby is asleep.
Everything's okay—
knowing even now
some fucker counts
the flies.

# I Am Told

I am told gravity insists.
So I lie ass flat on a green deck.

The sea comes at me like a sexual spurt.
I am my own bicuspid.

Bone white, a wave turns in,
hits steel like middle C.

A man moves his feet from my head,
says, I'll leave you alone.

I can never finish what they start.
I never have.

I find we pay attention to the center
of things. Girls bend

to wash their hair in the sink.
The receptacles are stuffed and overturned.

If the Aegean is good they do the route
four times a day.

We are all going away.
And what will be left?

Spit, a couple of words, someone's anger
turned out on a BMW, on an island

that closes shop in the winter,
and will not budge to remember

my presence or yours.
The sun will take care of that.

It is a clean history we imagine.

# The Power of Reasoning

My student said that people who say
they have good intentions are really
just covering up wrongdoings.

My mother said that if her only son
moved away and decided never to see her again,
that if he were happy, well,
she would be too.

Happy people must be superior to sad.
Sad people might find darkness
on the corner,
rather than around, waiting
for them.

My friend said she gets by easier than most
so she is happy.
In California they have removed the bump,
smoothed the turn of her nose.
In California, she said, they think young.

Children are happy.
They are younger than most.
None of them lose face
when they cry.
They lose hats and gloves
because they are not attached
to the body, self,
really.

# In Search of Restitution

## 1

There is a dread to being replaced.

Bulldozers pull up
their spare brick
and cinder block,
scoop down for another
part.

Buses turn their fancy asses
like accordions,
wheezing in for the next stop.
Blues bars are scoped
and cleaned for the 10 o'clock.

Buildings are just talk.


## 2

Finally,
the haunt of sulfur leaves you.

You begin to notice a climate change.
Mountains appear.
The sky is smaller.

You prepare for the desert:
fill your tank,
lock all your doors,
and remember,
*the greatest source of sorrow*
*is the belief in a single, enduring*
*personality.*

There you go. There you are.

# Incommunicado

Sorry pal, memory doesn't allow
for the capacious luxury of idle behavior.
It's work to call it all back.

*You go so far and then you stop.*

These feelings have no address on earth.

*Why do you stop?*

There should be more hands in photographs
with the ability to seep through the fine grain,
thrust their creamy palms onto my shoulders
and *give me a real good talkin' to* — redirect
the heat I have so often referred to as circumstance.

Signs of change confuse me.

In a car you think the telephone poles are moving.
They say this is an optical illusion, that you
are traveling past the poles.
They are stationary.
So how do you account for their presence
on the drive—
Remember them less?

Sounds rarely trouble me.
A scream is a holler,
a radio is a song,
a word is memorial.

I am here. I am at the window
convinced that the obscenity of this moment
is that it happens all at once.

*You sound hopeless.*

The girls across the way continue to paint
the narrow margins around their eyes
in spite of the man who circles their stove
with flaming cheese ... *take this and this.*

Two floors down the married couple glance up at me,
and with their faces:
*Please, say nothing.*

Power is peculiar.

I set flowers on the sill.
I know that if I do not split the shoots,
these birds of paradise will not open
their orange mouths.
In the wild it takes a turbulent wind or an animal
to separate the buds.
If it were up to them, well,
they would stay shut.

People demand a response.

The man across the way hangs his wash, pauses
to drink milk from the carton.
I begin to document his steps, revering
the wholesome routine of settling shirts
onto hangers — comparing often
how we spare ourselves pain.

I have great faith in the matter of fact,
in the quiet hesitation
for more, more words?

The silent rumble of color through glass
makes my tongue sore.

*But how does it make you feel?*

The man starts to vacuum the length of a room
as honorably as some farmer marking
fertile soil.
He pops a beer
in the middle of the afternoon.

I say I can feel the wet slap on my chin.

I have become as small as a syllable
of myself.
I try to find the place where I am tired,
where only a hand can speak
confidently.

*Is there something that might make you more comfortable?*

Rice bubbles on the rear flame.
I am amazed at how far steam treks.

Inside of a minute
what resembles a face in the window
changes to a hill,
then a cloud,
almost a perfect circle—

like breath testing its potential on a mirror.


*for Anne*

# Clearly Heaven

Lit by the canine quarter of a moon
the 36 bus draws
open its door

A lady with a honey-how-da-do smile
makes room for the guy without an eye

His torso moves like a mime:
CAN YOU HELP ME KEEP
MY PLACE?

Neon flicks for a stop
(quietly and uncensored)

A kid picks the remains of a scab—
that final effort to be soft

How raw the change for departure

How utterly slow
the window takes in

what stays

# This Is the Sound I Make

looking for the primates—
Above the starry heavens there are no bodies
to contend with.

Fire ants paralyze their prey.
In another life you watched them do it.

My sister says you can tame a wild sparrow,
feed it tuna from a free hand,
let it wrap its feet around your finger
like thread or floss, thin
and going away—
You remember heat
from the last time someone else turned your body.

The queen can produce 200 eggs a day.
Her sting is painful.

The orangutan has no tail.
He enjoys an orbit
of rope and space, takes
his sex all day in his hands,
after apples,
indifferently.

She goes off by herself
in time-lapsed photography.

# At a Distance

Sometime soon none of this will matter.
And outside
those birch trees bandaged
like race horses will probably be gone
or destroyed. So let's sit here, Mother,
in our sling chairs
and drink your decaffeinated coffee
in the family room,
while your stationary bicycle
remains stationary
and this house gives up
a little less.
Because you live alone

you think every sound is significant.
You say you can hear your pulse
palpitate in your wrist and neck.
I don't believe you.
You tell me you're scared to stay alone —
to be alone. You tell me you can hear
your dead parents' voices at night. Your mother
asking your father, *Is there someone at the door?*

Mother, can't you see what has happened?
Each day we die a little more.

# Talk about Daddy

When Bessie Smith sings about Daddy
she means a lover. But when I talk
about Daddy, I mean a man full of gin,
who once told me, *You don't need to coddle
any guy's balls,*
*they don't break, y'know?*
Maybe Bessie would have thought better
of my old man
than I did. You see,
all I have wanted is to have him hold me
and tell me
something simple. Maybe about the rain,
what it looks like in the kitchen.
The way it feels, Daddy,
the quiet air. You wanted
to keep things simple. Rib-cord spreads
to match naked white walls, Kansas at dusk
hung in the living room.
You told me God took the girl
you married during the war. You said
that was okay — the way
you missed her, the way I still see
her face, the face I've never seen,
shaped loose in the spills of water
on the porch.
Aunt Sully says,
*People don't need to talk.*
Daddy, I have fucked
and loved all at the same time—
the way this match turns
gold, before I let it
go, not expecting anymore
the color of blue or the smell
of sulfur
in the bathroom.

# Small Town

The screen door
swells in the heat:
gnat,
wasp.

My mother vacuums
around my feet:
bone,
nail.

Milk dries
in the base of a bowl:
fruit,
grain.

My mother sits
to remove the pins
from a new shirt:
buttonhole,
blade.

A lady on TV
pulls out a gun:
scalp,
sky.

# Biography

What happened yesterday
What is happening now

If I tell you
Is not the truth

Truth is an image
Michigan is a mitten

The shape of my hand
Is a small map

Four creases below knuckle
Is my mother's home

The body has many sides
I move between

The red slats of a snow fence
My shoulder blade touches only one side

Three steps forward
One back

The family gets smaller
When we talk on the phone

Heads develop first in a Polaroid
A green curve comes next

The landscape between us
Is taped on my refrigerator door

The soul always opening
To the unnerving hum

Of this and that

# Hopper's Girl

But you are never that girl,
Hopper's girl, on my wall.
Naked in a green chair, she sits
resting her elbows on her knees,
hands locked together, her auburn head
turned; I can't see her face.
1926? I wonder
if there is anything outside
that window worth the sadness
of ordered space.

There is a lamp too large
for the table, and above the dresser
is a painting — I can't make out the landscape.
Strange to see her wearing shoes
when she could just as easily be barefoot
at 11 A.M. in the nude.
Could this be you?
Someone's recognition in yellow
of what might have been

were it possible to dream an old lady
young. But you are never that girl,
Hopper's girl. You are a woman
who hides her money under her brassieres,
who prays the rosary and swears
in her sleep, who tells me I'm
a good girl, that there are buffalo and jobs in Iowa.
You are an old woman
who sits on the edge of the tub
soaking her feet, watching the bitter salts
dissolve and settle at the bottom.


*for my grandmother*

# Ponder the Motion

# Ponder the Motion

We should move the swing to the front of the porch.

We could see more —
our souls
would rest parallel to the cars
to the trees
to the sidewalk
where the boy lobs papers
on all the other porches.

We would always be the same distance apart,
from the boy, the trees,
from the cars.
We would be happy on this porch.

Yes,
but what would our consciences think
of such a move?

Oh,
they would sit inside us
taking it all in
and after a week or a month
they would tell us exactly
how they felt.
They would make us pick up
the four books
swelled and water-stained
on the railing.

They would make us go inside.

# Whisper

Whisper: one two three four. Breathe in through
        your mouth.
Now softer, say: won-too-three-faar, one-two-three-four.
Faster: onetwothreefour, wontothrfr. Say e: E E E.

I have gone past what you see in your eyes
when I look at them.

There are small hairs on your lungs that keep
bacteria out.
Ahhhhhh. Once more. Ahhhhhhhhhh.
If you're looking for the tonsils— Gone.
Forced removal.
Now you are looking at the place where they were.

If I hadn't given you to memory there would be no pain.

There are two kinds of infection. One, you see, just runs
its course. And the other can be treated.

Choice means you prefer one thing rather than another.
Out my window,
in the opposite apartment, three women
are drinking pink champagne. Now what if one decides,
in the midst of a toast, that she would have preferred
sparkling cider? Then what?

Sometimes your face would fall a little
when I spoke.
I would watch the sun land on your stomach,
then hit the very floor of your room.

Whisper: one two three four. Breathe in through
        your mouth.
Now softer, say: won-too-three-faar, one-two-three-four.
Faster: onetwothreefour, wontothrfr. Say e: E E EXILE.

# In Order to Get Up

she must paint her toenails
red, put on black leotards,
a tee shirt cut in a V,
divert her stare to a compact mirror,
tip of her nose, her lips,
pluck small hairs.

Leaves fall to the ground,
sound like someone passing by,
groundhog chews a cigarette pack
tossed after a party.

These are the distractions
that jerk open the door,
suck her to the street to dance.
Her fists shake,
the pitch of leaves drops like olive pits
from her mouth—

people you have loved.

# The Intractable Lover

24,000 feet in the air,
clouds, the continental divide,
4 window exits over the wings.

It's easy to be alive
when you know
everything comes from something real.

Pull down on the mask
to start the oxygen flow.
Down there,

the farms are simply schisms
of soil and crop.
God is in the rain

on the cockpit windshield
being exquisitely pushed
from one side to the other.

# Elsewhereness

I have tied the curtains in knots
to see the people below, and I know there are people
who have their names in dictionaries.
I am the orange that sits next to me,
pocked and somewhat empty.
I am the "o" that starts the word "orange,"
that uses the knife to cut four slices.
Distance is language spent too easily.
It is how I feel asleep on the bathroom floor
as I hold my ribs like a package from the butcher.
You said you didn't want to put out
and I tell you intimacy is kind.
I moved my bed to the living room to lay down
and hear the voices outside. Instead,
I hear the wind, plug in my fan
that hums automatically.

Now in the attic I can press my hand to the window,
touch the tree limbs like bones.
Elsewhere people fuck.
The lady down the block shoves her hoe into the garden
methodically. Sadness is a lot like this—
each perfunctory gesture is a word spent.
It is the color of this floor. Red,
or is it cranberry? You might call it maroon
and you might be right.
You asked me to say all that I would say.
Sometimes I peel off the splits at the end of my hair,

and when I get four in one strand I call it a ladder.
I have a fear of my foot falling asleep at the movies.
I hope I never run out of paper products.
I like to make love
the way I like this room
that lodges only two chairs
and a telescope without a lens.
And what I understand is the dirt space
between each wood slat, the way it feels
under my fingernails.

# Under the Volcano

If only we could cure my neurosis everything would be
      all right.

I am melodramatic about rejection. You think we
      should examine
our awkwardness in the place it happens, and I think
      of a story
about a lover who was seven hours late for a dinner party:

> When he arrived he went to bed.
> His girlfriend pitched her cocktail
> at a mirror above his head. She
> heard the smash—*I have gone too far*—
> dropped her body like a scrap.

With us speech runs rampant in time. Grapes plunged
      into mouths,
club soda poured over heads, "don't touch me" shouted over
"leave it alone," meshed in with "I shouldn't be here. I am."

We talk about pain like an invention. A strange idea
perfected, patented—who did it? where? and what for?
Someone plays I-grieve-so-great-I-can't-discuss-it,
and the other wants to know what we should do.

The one who shouts the loudest hears
a mallet bong 435 pounds to the top—a bell rings—
we are located in a room we have begun to rely on.

We have simple rules:
When the phone rings we do not interrupt the argument.
We try to leave our bodies out of it.

# The Good Life

We take each other in the car,
in a public arena we call HIGHWAY.
You take it peripherally
by map, landmark,
and movement.
Going west I take
the open road
in memory.
Fourth gear. Staccato.
Three trucks take a look down.
Salt Lake is in the rearview.

This is how it is
in California, early
eucalyptus, late July.
Cars pass.

No one really knows the angle
of your body
taking the turns,
how you see
the space between —
rather than the line,
passing,
giving history imagination.

No one will ever know
where you go
when you go inside
where it happens
to keep happening.
They may offer you a ride,
or a ticket:
punch on destination,
punch on exit.
Someone you don't know
may offer you
a separate, deliberate
prayer to acquiesce.

# Indian Style

This room is for all of us, interlopers,
voices trying to replicate the loon or the chickadee
as we lie on a brown sheet and understand gravity.

Everything in love is a trade-off.

Our touch takes its design
from two marionettes that hang from the ceiling.
Nothing can move them away.
One week ago a dog was let loose in the country.

If we think before we act,
then we lift our hands more than once.
If we do not,
we go into love uncharted
like the childhood exercise
where the pencil never lifts from the page.

No one gets up to leave.

# Fear

I remember everything.
My knees drawn up to my mouth
pull me into a circle
for you.

There is no distance that cannot be understood.

Three chicks across the way,
enamored of wine and pretty wrists,
are like the weight of envelopes.

I kiss off the sax player on the stereo
and get my time easy
as a ticket passed from hand
to hand, tossed—
*who we are* into a can.

I am afraid
of the past tense
when you look at me,
that *here*,
the aftermath of getting
will end with the stroke of your thumb
on my palm, moving
to the forefinger,
to the index,
to the nail,
grinding down like sunlight
on cuticle and cloud.

Now, who could argue with that.

# Angels on the Ceiling

Like skin they come to the Aegean
to be generous with their quarter mile out.

Out there, they bob gray—
*Ella, ella, delphins,*

ladles pulling up salt,
releasing, circulating turns . . .

They are like our small contemporary selves—
of the earth, lying on limestone, sweating.

What we see when we observe is shy memory,
sediments of color, self, sin.

Like a fingerprint we press ourselves
to go back to the origin of the involuntary

house, lover, tree.
Nepenthe, nepenthe, nepenthe.

# Fieldworker

In a borrowed room, on plaid sheets,
in a bed small enough for a child,
everything is less familiar.

With electric fences almost invisible,
and stretched like fishing line by her side—
Does she look up from the tassel

before she makes the pull?
This is what I want to know.
I burn a candle with someone else's memorabilia,

someone else's nightclub matches.
I watch a cylinder shape rise on the wall
like an unusual lifeline, phosphorescent,

and yellowed. She opens her hand,
peeling back each finger like a rind.
Her palm is stalk stained, rogue colored,

pastoral. She does not know I think I can
hear her dream, a delicate snap,
and she removes the end of a string bean.

All day she is the green, the designated
female rows that go on for miles, split sometimes
into halves and quarters like fruit.


*to Ginny Ruth Threefoot*

# Evidence for a Love Poem

Trees are talk.
My steps are the ideas I walk with.

Someone puts food in the tank,
a Black Mollie forgets another Black Mollie.

His back is a gulf,
each vertebra a line extending.

Hair on earlobes:
he is a mammal.

Water prills into a drain,
returns to a tiny ball.

A column of sun blasts her eyes.
The left arm juts forward.

She has oxidized.

She is the color of field
when her spine bends.

# What You Said

I have always thought
that what I touch I can have.

Being lovers meant we could feel
each other's flesh without permission.

Being separate was different
from alone. You said I had the face

of an angel, but I know
there are angels better than me.

I thought what made me separate
was the way I could see smoke rising

from a lamp—if I looked long enough
I could see your right hip, the bone

pronounced in the light. I move
in a room I have made less

and less comfortable. I've taken
the curtains down to try and make

sense of what you said about wanting,
having, and losing—all the same thing.

You said it was because of time
that we feel them in different stages.

Is this time too slow?
If I touch my calf right now, notice

the true color of my skin, lift my hand,
is it all the same moment?

If I see myself in the window,
what have I lost?

# Architecture of an Affair

Not much furniture.
Huge white windowsills to sit on.

A grocery store nearby.

One person uses a three-way mirror to see you.
The other leaves the door ajar.

One says the light on the floor is mellifluous.
The other speaks with her hands.

They start to name everything.
The ring she wears from the Black Hills is familiarity.

They own the same kind of car by coincidence.

How little to expect
it ever to be different than the best.

One stands in the kitchen.
The other studies the underbelly of a spoon.

A moth sticks to the windowpane.

# Bodies Subject to Its Action

# 3rd Coast Café

Inside all the faces, all the change,
everything is in order, clearly marked,
correctly placed, American.
We keep all the bills in the drawer,
facing toward you, to the left.
When you arrive you seat yourself.
We give you a name according to the painting
above you. This morning
"Skull and Book" is a mother and son
who pay their bill from a small safe.
He props up the steel box to his ear
to listen to the world tell him:
three times right, twice left, right,
stop, and then open.
"Self-Portrait" has a baby and a friend.
The child teethes on mandelbread
and does not know how to suppress her words.
In the middle of things, the middle of the room,
transition is a strawberry blonde who has no name.
She paints her nails, holds them above
a coffee cup, and waits for change,
the steam to moisten her fingertips.
She makes a fist to look at what she's done.
"Reclining Nude" turns on a brass lamp
to see his words upright and lit: *Brie, apple, decaffeinated.*

Something must return.
Something must remain pure, spontaneous,
make us feel more important, less significant,
more insecure, sure, singular.
The Air must be taken, passed,
for something more than language
or the fraudulence of polite behavior.

Look again, look at your water glass to the right.
See it for a second time in the window,
once removed, reflected, all of us,
delightfully real.

This is how we get it right.
We clean the ashtrays with discarded napkins.
We measure the baguettes by the length of a blade.
To make the tuna we use pepper, lemon, and mayonnaise.
If you order the house wine we give you
a smidge more than the Bordeaux.
If your lover falls in love with someone else,
become friends. Go away. Keep coming back.
Memorize a conversation you've overheard,
"This is a difficult time in my life."
There is a system to everything.
You realize you do not know how it works.
If "Still Life with Radishes" orders a croissant,
you must heat it.
Serve the knife before the butter and marmalade.
Carry all your accoutrements in the palm of your hand,
and let them, let them take it.

# Reckoning with the Sheep

You wrote to tell me the black-eyed susans in New Mexico
blink in the wind keeping their stories to themselves.

I write back to say break time in the fields means
a collapsible cup of water,
fifteen minutes to feel the earth,
to rinse corn rash off your thighs, to imagine
the roots of the stalks as ruby-colored birds' feet.

> *Twenty-five seconds and they're gone*
> *to the other side of the hill.*

I am being evasive, withholding information, keeping
bait on the hook perhaps.

> *I can't get to them. Barbed wire.*
> *Can't get past the black snouts to the white,*
> *faces, to their eyes.*

I am always on the edge of getting there.
I try to remember what makes them stay.
What makes them go.
There is no clarity in memory.
This must be the conversation we are always on
the verge of continuing.

Your hair is probably auburn from the sun.
I do not remember it that way.
What I think of is volcanic sand, a snorkeler
giving me a shell,
something to take back, away with me.
I keep it in a bag, later, realize
a creature is alive.
I cannot keep it. Something is moving.

> *I try to remember what will make it stay.*

Theory, I write you, is much more powerful in memory.

This is fact: people were smaller in the beginning.
They had a window to the right of the door.
Their houses were made of sandstone.

This is explanation: People go away.

Fieldwork, I write, has everything to do with timing,
it is the rhythm,
the pollen in the air,
the rhythm
pollen in the air
rhythm
the pollen in the air
rhythm
tassel
tassel
pollen in the air
pollen in the air
hand over hand
over hand
over hand
over hand
pollen in the air
over hand
over hand.

# The Waitress Purports Change

Pick it up.
Do you want? Anything?
Make it fast.
Turn it over. Once you say *what* the sky
crystallizes into a red
columbine, pollution, late October,
November, Day of the Dead.
A white rind, a cloud finally
forms and severs the antennae of the John Hancock.
At exactly 12 stops from Division
you are near north, lakeside, Chicago.
It is nothing like you expected.
A girls plays the flute on the platform,
waits for the south train, doesn't seem to mind
how time will take her away from you
as you step down the out stairs, lower level, Loyola.
A woman sets her poodle on top of a public phone.
A boy offers you a shine and a cigarette,
the rest he's sacrificed to the el train.
Nothing comes back how you want it.

*Saucer, you know, on top of cup,*
*on top of saucer, spoons in the middle,*
*napkins under the arm.*

You are surprised by your own safety.
You tell everyone there have been strangers
here before you, and you
are changing into something else.
Clear it away.
Turn it right side up.
Stack it. You can handle it.
There is no past here, here
in the center of the white

saucer, brown spill like a birthmark.
We always turn to our opposites.
Once you say *why* a man looks into the chrome
of a public phone, paints
an anonymous nosebleed on his face.
Before you know it
he is gone,
with your speculation,
to connect, through the tunnel,
westbound and waiting.
What you call interference
is the powerless echo of human noise,
the usual, the attempt
to say, "Transfer, please."

# Betrayal

Episodically, if you look far enough ahead
something fails.

    Holding back is nothing at all.

*It will happen again.*
Tomorrow a biosatellite may be put in the air.
And today an empty gourd holds French bread
sliced perfectly into threes and fours.

Put your ears on some language.
"I don't want to eat alone."

The rind of the Brie is like milky skin.
The sky is a combination of cornucopia,
gray, and Beaujolais.

"You want more? Okay."

    Behind each volatile *no problem,*
    *get right to it, in a second,*
    *we have no more, sorry we're out,* smile—

familiarity is never a choice.

# Nothing Passes Away

We itch the underside of the knee
Belly up in corn rash.

We piss in the fields
Find ourselves a tall one.

In the morning all you hear is the incessant ping
Of grasshoppers flicking from one leaf to the next.

We wear scarves tied in the back
To cover our foreheads from the sun.

In the distance like a horizon,
A man's shoulder blade is a white line of lotion.

We start early and when we end
Our palms are the color of sky.

We smell like wind.
We take the bus back.

The animals are a perfect brown.
Cows grazing their slow dedication to the land,

As if everyone could live there.

# The Integrity of Pigeons

When I can no longer hear the oboe,
when the piano fails to separate,
restrict the movements in my heart—
I will put lard on my face

and press it to stone,
see my cheeks blot
a lithograph on newsprint,
the blue veins below my eyes

will not appear. If I choose
*not* to sketch the strands
around my face
I will be the bald man

who sits across from the china store
and watches the pigeons perched
on eaves, their integrity
their lavender necks,

the way they twitch them without bother,
without need for recognition.
If I were to show that man my print
I would not tell him

this is a woman—it is me.
I would sit with him
outside of the china store,
pigeon shit on the window—

We would look at all the inaccuracies together:
reflections, the wooden bench,
our shoes, skulls, and jawbones,
that somehow we have wished were different.

# Andante

It's hard to resist affection when you're tired,

when someone you have loved touches your face,
curtains the hair from your forehead.

Perfect, the gray municipality
of a train station.
Marvelous climate for painful memories,
a finger wavering from the barrel of a glass,
a taut mouth waiting for the service
of a word, or the private laws of choice
that seem to languish
in this marble auditorium
dedicated to motion.

It's all you can do to stand still,

to stop the stoic behavior
of your feet
following instinct, following
each other.

Our there, darling, is just out there
with the rest of us . . .
perusing the insolent
and fair sky that begs
its color from the moon.

Nothing we have ever done
can equal the clarity
in the posture of wooden pews,
that momentarily,
in their exactness, let me
leave you.

# February 10th

If this is the world,
the old woman in a pink muu-muu
can shake her throw rug
on the corner of Dodge and Market.

If love is interrogation,
then what questions do I ask?
If all we know about each other
is how we behave, what we decide to tell—

then what is silence? I don't need
to know that woman's name, the reason
she parts her hair on the side,
the shape of her hips underneath her dress,

whether or not a pattern of paper peels
off her kitchen wall. For a short frame,
a city block, she is the world
on February 10th. She asks

absolutely nothing of me
as she turns and simply rests
the striped rug on the porch
to air.

# Sitting in the Kitchen Sink, Therefore I Am

This is where it starts again.
This is where the quiet is delivered
by the unquiet—
iridescent howls, water on the outside lip
of the drain seeps down.

This is the place that hears
bottles scraped up by forklift trucks.
This is the 14th floor
where the sky is lit up
by other people's apartments.
The moon is accurately placed:
Up there.

Sometimes we suppose ourselves so small,
so improperly sized,
that our past becomes us less.

# Autonomy

A bouillon cube burns at the bottom of a pot.
The steeple peals another religious song.

After 44 years the portrait artist
drops her work in the trash.
Someone's coffee grounds topple
over nose and mouths.

Tonight the little black boys are spiffed
in half-ass tuxes, courting a shine
from a tall man's boots,
for a buck, for the chance
to spit on the stomach of a reptile.

Down the street the Korean lady takes,
takes to heart the cool breeze frosting the cellophane
on her roses as she bends down
to place a leaf back on a tree.

Two guys flick on their battery-operated geraniums
to see their faces in mine.
The neighborhood can lady threatens
to whip out her tit, press
it to the window of Z's,
like newsprint
or grief.

How manageable time is,
facing west, ruthless in my own
commodity of fear.
I want to feel the implosion of white
apartment light, pluck
the lonely pulp, and let it fall
to where it is clearly animal,
nonviolent, sort of sexy, tumid—

Such exact concentration.
An eternity for a second.

# Bodies Subject to Its Action

In the early evening, compunction is a window
at a slant reflected on the wall. An ex-lover

is the lock you want to turn 180 degrees
open. The new lover, like an orange cat,

follows the line to the apex, discovering things
under the A on the ground where stairs meet porch.

On a highway an opossum's kidney bulges
perpendicular to the dotted lines—

In linear time we are always in triangles.
To keep whole we spit our distance into the vortex

where we take off, take off, take off our clothes
like we did, like we do, like we will.

So we close one eye, lose a dimension,
never hear the crow caw the same way.

We belong to nothing.
Something is lost when geese move in formation.

# In the Same Breath

The neighbor boy is being paid to kill the dandelions
on the widow's front lawn.

We're out on Highway 218 in your lover's car, pretending
it's natural to want to
hear wind.

It is negligent to speak just now.

Who'd have thought the widow would also pay the boy
to cover her windows with brown paper bags,
that she preferred not to see.

I mean here we are in your lover's car, evaluating
landscape: strong cow, average silo,
green field.

The boy spits, furls back his hair,
chucks weeds into a sack.

*Easy being animal, isn't it?*
*Easy to want more.*

Your thumbnail lingers on my chin.

I think of the boy just now.
How we do what we are asked.

# Paranoia

**1**

When we recover this time you spoke of,

did you mean dream time
or simply the moment before
you catch yourself falling, and fortunately,
upright in your bed,
are consciously saved.

Let's say it is real, and you've
come back (like the men who lug

tree limbs to a white trailer
after a storm)

to get me. Say there were others too,

lovers, who given
a modicum of choice, replaced

their eyebrows with lichen,
camouflaged their mouths
with kindling, hollowed out acorns
for ears, and belched their torsos
from the unresolved trunk
of a gutted oak—

upon hearing of your return.

**2**

I have not forgotten you.
Still, I call back the identifiable

scent of your skin.
"Time now?" you ask.

And because this is dream,
I have no foresight.
Situations just occur, happen.

You bring me to a pool.

I notice the lines on your knuckles,
circular as tree rings.
In the blue water, roped off
into lanes, women raise their arms synchronously,
then slowly, through the weight of water,
I see their legs, knees, calves, and finally
their toes, which they dip
like tea leaves into the chlorine
haze.

They beckon me closer.

And because this is dream,
memory bends—

my actions have no consequences.

# Diminishing Returns

We acclimate ourselves
to the disharmony

of a rented room,
as we watch the east sun

pull apart the chipped texture
of a porch door,

swollen from the heat.
9:02 and we are closer

to the moon. Even though
we keep moving,

our bodies are still.
Beyond this point,

beauty deliberates
just how long

we can afford to pay
heed to a cat

licking the fallen skin
of an onion, while

two sparrows douse
their heads in the navel

of a puddle,
and you, up all night,

hold vigil
over the sound of water

offing itself
from the picket-fence

shape of their wings.

# Never a Singular Happening

We learn fast how to manufacture pain.
*Grief,* she said, *is a moment when there is nothing else*
                                        *but the past.*
Perhaps,
            this is why the dragonfly pays such close attention.

    It must know that impact includes an aftershock, as it
bales on down to Lake Pontchartrain.

*What we want,* she said, *negotiates who we are.*

You are right little-girls-at-the-beach-with-your-daddy
to beg your safety from *all that wet.* The world is undertow

                                        and sandbar.

Deftly,
            the dragonfly trolls below my other ear, reminding
me with its helicopter breath that

                        your head hit pavement two times,
                        the car rolled five, dropped fifteen feet.

*No one,* she said, *gives back their dead.* We bury them close to
home
                    so we know where they are, how far down
they have gone

                                        without us.

We bend to grace the shoulder of topsoil with our cartons of
scrupulous plants, orange geraniums.

*This,* she said, *is our selective distance:* the smell of dirt,

the Celsius temperature on a bank sign, the anonymous
dragonfly that moves and moves to make its life seem longer.

# When the Band Plays

From a skylift ride at Aquarena,
a place where pigs are taught to dive,
children calculate wishes,
aim pennies at the eyes
of a sleeping alligator—
I see the olive mechanical skin
of a mermaid I want to touch.

*Life is a beach*
written on the side
of a slam-dance bar in Texas
makes it less
what they are doing, the punks,
as they thrash themselves into
and out of each other.
I kiss a lover
and take my own
time to notice the silence
between sets as if that
were enough to live with.

Across the street,
a woman sits on her porch
while I decide she is not lonely,
that her life is full of mystery.
She is hiding something,
the shade in her living room pulled
down, white skirt over knees.
Her fifty-eight-year-old body
is lovely in the sunlight,
in the ordinary, in what is not
ours.

*for Pauline*

327 154